HOW TO
SCALE
your stupid
LAW FIRM

HOW TO
SCALE
your stupid
LAW FIRM

Hamid Kohan

Unstoppable CEO Press

Hamid Kohan
Hkohan@LegalSoftSolution.com
www.LegalSoftSolution.com

[How To Scale Your *Stupid* Law Firm] Hamid Kohan —1st ed.
ISBN: 978-1-955242-32-5

DEDICATION

I'd like to dedicate this book to my amazing family, my wife who has been there for me through thick and thin, and especially my two outstanding boys Bobby & Shayan who will be future partners of the Kohan & Kohan law group, following the completion of their legal studies. Their contribution and commitment to this venture has been tremendous to say the least and I look forward to assisting them in scaling their own firm.

EPIGRAPH

You may ask why I decided to name this book "How to Scale Your Stupid Law Firm". Well, this is the most common question I get asked when consulting with firms nationwide and as I dive into the innerworkings of their operations we solve the problems of dealing with "stupid lead generation, stupid marketing, and stupid training courses" for their staff.

INTRODUCTION

After working hand-in-hand with many incredibly successful high-tech companies over the years, I've come across an excellent opportunity to work and assist the legal industry in benefiting from recently available technologies that allow for the optimization, expansion, and ability to streamline law practices.

I started off working with a handful of law practices locally and soon realized the greater need to assemble a team of experts in a panoply of different roles, such as Business Development, Marketing, and Operations. Combined with several innovative technologies, we've developed a thought-out and result-oriented one-stop shop for law practices nationwide.

This book is a summary of techniques and implementations that have helped hundreds of law firms build successful law practices and optimize and expand consistently. Several firms that have adopted these methods have scaled 3X a year, and they're just getting started!

I hope this book will be as beneficial for every reader as it has been for our network of clients we have worked with and scaled with over the past year.

CONTENTS

CHAPTER 01

Practice Challenges—The Attorney's Struggle

My many years of working with a wide variety of practice areas and with law firms of varying sizes has allowed me to detect a multitude of problems that these firms face internally and operationally. However, depending on the size of these firms, these problems were either detrimental to their practice or had an acute impact on the firm.

To better break down my step-by-step guide to scaling your law firm, I have categorized law firms as solo practitioners, medium-sized firms, and large firms.

Solo Practitioners (1–6 staff)

The biggest problem solo firms face is increasing the number of clients they retain without spending an absurd amount of money, essentially "sampling" different lead generation companies. Like everyone else, they want more cases, yet they don't have capital to front and ultimately can't generate cases at a reasonable cost. Because of the lack of budget and proper appropriation of funds, they struggle to grow their practice, and more importantly, they can't find out how to scale while keeping their costs low.

They look for alternative ways of getting cases, often resorting to using their social media platforms or getting referrals from large firms across different practice areas. Mostly, referrals become the main source of new cases for these law practices and since this strategy is almost 100% risk free, many believe it is the key to becoming the next big law firm.

The second problem for solo firms is learning how to manage the business operations and learning how to properly delegate mundane work to others in the firm. The law practice owners are doing everything they know how to, however, due to their lack of experience and education with business management, the firm begins juggling multiple things at a time and often dropping the ball.

They look at large law firms and ask, how are they doing it? What is their marketing budget and strategy? How can they juggle handling so many cases and still manage to make all this money?

The solo practitioners think there's some sort of magic recipe that allows firms to grow. In fact, there is no magic recipe. It's a mix of a lot of time invested, risk management, and simultaneous hard work. Not to mention that these law firms are willing to try different management methods which eventually leads to a large amount of case settlements every year. Additionally, they begin investing some of the income back into the business rather than just hiring more staff or spending unreasonable amounts on marketing without any promise of improvement on the practice management infrastructure fundamentals.

Solo practitioner firms search for other attorneys that practice in the same area, went to the same school, operate in the same state, yet they're making $300,000 a month, while the solo practitioner is only making $20,000 a month, and they don't understand why.

Medium-Sized Law Practices (6–20 Staff)

The biggest problem that medium-sized law firms face is growth. How do they get to the next level? They look at other large firms and wonder, "How can I get that big?"

When you look closely, you find that the problem is a lack of structure and infrastructure. The law practice owner has hired 10 or 15 people, and each person is fulfilling their role. However, they lack structure. The job responsibilities are not defined, and the workflow is not set up. They also lack the required technology to grow. Basically, they need a complete remodeling of the firm's operational structure.

They need to make sure they have allocated their resources in the right place, otherwise, it leads to various degrees of confusion.

For example, the attorneys are not focusing on practicing the law, the case managers are not focused on building the value of the case, and the list goes on. Rather than having everyone in the law firm focus on one key area, we see the flip side of that where the attorney, the case manager, and law practice owner all do a little bit of intake, a little bit of case management, and a little bit of document collection.

There isn't a standard process, and there are no performance metrics. Which leads the law practice owner to be oblivious to how many cases the firm is signing up, selling, or referring.

They don't know which questions to ask to assist in making management or growth decisions. They don't know the numbers that drive the firm, and they don't know what to do next. They often have no facts, nor data in which to base their decisions on.

Everyone in the firm is working hard, everybody is busy, yet there is no steady growth.

It's unclear what the profitability of the firm is because there is no financial analysis. The financial information about the firm is limited to bookkeeping. It's almost like they're balancing a checkbook and not running a law firm operation.

Instead of having proactive operations, they are reactive. If money is coming in, it must have been a good month and they're happy that they are doing well, but if there is no money coming in, it's been a bad month and suddenly the staff or lead generation company is to blame. The real problem lies in the law firm not knowing why it has been a good month or why it has been a poor month!

They have no control over their analytics. In other words, medium-sized firms don't know how many cases they need to settle, how many cases they need to close, and what their net attorney fees per case need to be to be profitable. They get what they can, cash their checks, and repeat the cycle of overspending.

Everything is done based on daily routines. There are no set budgets, structures, performance metrics, or other avenues to signal red flags ahead of time. Owners react to the current situation because many of them believe it is possible to plan for the future without accurate data. Track and understand your firm analytics, such as Caseloads per staff (Sample Below).

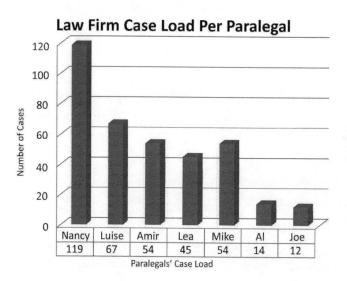

The managing attorney ends up working more than anyone else in the firm. They're doing everything themselves, or if they aren't single handedly doing it, they somehow find a way to involve themselves in every minute detail of the practice. They're not holding their staff or specific departments accountable, and most of the wins and losses present in the firm are chalked up to good days or bad days, when in reality, a streamlined operation does not allow for such inconsistency.

This lack of structure and control over the numbers generates tremendous stress for the owners, and many decide that they don't want to grow. They quickly become content with where they are at. All they see is that growth means their life will get harder and complacency begins to overwhelm. To avoid that excess stress and worry, they decide to limit themselves and instead of trying to grow the law practice to the next level, they try to maintain the level they are at.

Of course, they're making more money than they were as a solo practitioner, but they believe it's not enough to justify all the frustration that accompanies growth.

Nothing is predictable, and sometimes success hinges on luck. But sometimes, luck favors the prepared and many attorneys are just simply not prepared. Everyone's hoping they will get lucky with a contingency case like personal injury or employment. That one case will generate an amazing seven-figure revenue, and they'll be happy until the pain and misery starts over two years later but to truly succeed in this industry, you need to track and understand your law firm's analytics. Below is an example of tracking where your cases are coming from.

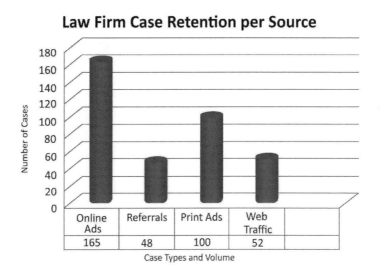

Law Firm Case Retention per Source

	Online Ads	Referrals	Print Ads	Web Traffic	
Number of Cases	165	48	100	52	

Case Types and Volume

Large Firms (20+ Staff)

Large firms often have a combination of problems faced by solo practitioners and medium-sized firms. They also don't have a meaningful, valuable reporting system and when they do, they lack an individual inside the firm that can analyze their data and give a forecast on the direction, growth, and potential cost reductions.

Large firms may have a lot of money, but they also carry a lot of dead weight, due to lack of control of their organization. This issue is quite the opposite for solo or medium-sized firms who often have the managing attorney micro-managing everybody's work and not allowing individuals to become an expert in their role through trial and error. At a large firm, they assume everybody is working hard and getting a lot done because the law firm sees success, however luck and being at the right place at the right time has a lot to play in "feeling successful", rather than actually being successful.

It goes back to accountability. When this firm gets big enough, there isn't as much loyalty. A firm of 300 employees doesn't have the same level of loyalty from their employees as a solo or medium sized firm would have. This is a great chart to track division of your firm cases based on the type of cases your firm is retaining and how to balance your resources.

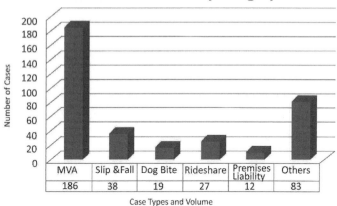

Law Firm Case Load By Category

MVA	Slip &Fall	Dog Bite	Rideshare	Premises Liability	Others
186	38	19	27	12	83

Case Types and Volume

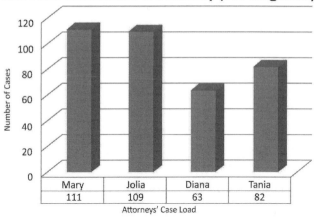

Law Firm Case Load Per Attorney (Pre-Litigation)

Mary	Jolia	Diana	Tania
111	109	63	82

Attorneys' Case Load

Large firms don't explore enough new law practice development opportunities, which limits their growth. They become dinosaurs and lack innovation in their practice.

When they come to me, they're looking to expand their practice into other areas or other states. They want to diversify and expand. In all other industries, when a company becomes large enough and has the budget, they start looking at acquisitions, and want to acquire a larger piece of the pie. In the legal field, this is a foreign concept.

I was one of the first to introduce the concept of buying other firms. This means acquiring solo practitioners, acquiring competitors, and purchasing the contact databases of attorneys who are near retirement.

But many large firms are not talking about searching for multiple avenues to expand and grow their firm. Attorneys attempt to create everything from scratch. If you have the funds and network, I recommend purchasing a few smaller firms to grow and utilize their contact database.

Law Firm Mergers

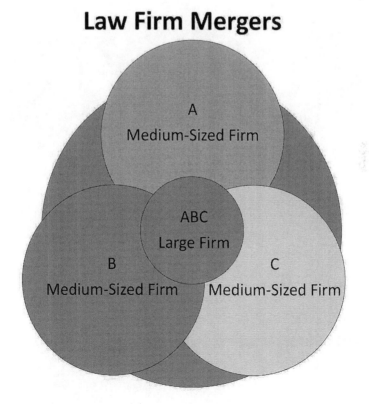

Traditionally, just like in the medical industry, when attorneys reach the end of their practice, they begin to wind down, get rid of staff, and close the door on new business. After years of blood, sweat, and tears, many attorneys feel content with their public service and forget that they have built a gold mine of client-attorney relationships; many of whom will need to find new attorneys to trust.

In other industries, that doesn't happen, company owners don't think about retiring. Instead, they try to position the company for acquisition and capitalize on the relationships they've built over the years.

Law Firm Aquisitions

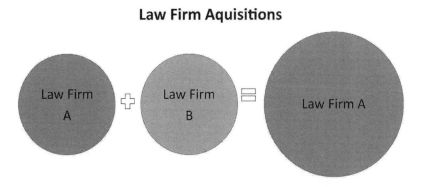

Another problem in big firms is that innovation in their practice becomes extremely difficult because the mindset and the culture are not there. Any new ideas get rejected, with several key members resisting change and surfing on their current success.

Another important thing to keep in mind when building a large firm is acknowledging that you will have a higher cost per case in comparison to medium or smaller law firms. The reason being that as law firms grow and they increase their revenue, money becomes less of a worry and attorneys are willing to shell out large sums of cash to continue acquiring cases. For example, if the cost to acquire a new client is $1,500 in a medium-sized firm, that same acquisition could cost $3,500 in a large firm because they can afford it. Because large firms are not as desperate nor are they living on as tight a budget as small firms, they don't look at costs as closely as their smaller counterparts. Every time they retain a new case, they become content, but they don't calculate what their CPA (Cost per Case Acquisition) is, what it takes to settle that case, or how many cases they need to settle in a year to maximize profits.

Larger firms become sloppy with their numbers as they start to ignore monitoring performance metrics and disregard their standards.

I always tell these clients that even if you have millions of dollars in the bank, it doesn't mean you can buy dollar bills for $1.50. You used to want to buy dollar bills for $0.85. Now you're willing to get them for $1.50. What changed? Your account balance, while everything else stays the same?

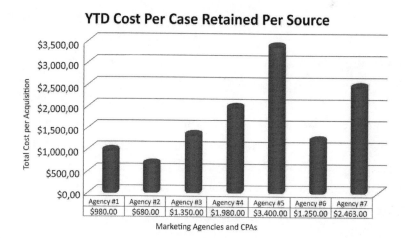

YTD Cost Per Case Retained Per Source

	Agency #1	Agency #2	Agency #3	Agency #4	Agency #5	Agency #6	Agency #7
	$980.00	$680.00	$1.350.00	$1.980.00	$3.400.00	$1.250.00	$2.463.00

Marketing Agencies and CPAs

Staffing Problems

Large firms believe they have the correct numbers in place to make the right decisions, but within the legal industry, that skill set is not common. So, owners hire a COO, a CFO, a CEO, or a CTO from other fields like finance, insurance, or medical to do the numbers. But just because they were successful in other industries doesn't mean they understand the law practice. So, they try to run a law practice like a mortgage company, but the metrics don't match.

> *There is a major shortage of highly skilled operators in the legal industry.*

In most other law practices, a CFO or a CTO from one industry can move to another industry and get the same types of results. The same strategies that work in those industries don't necessarily work in a law firm. So this creates a major shortage of highly skilled financial operators in the legal industry.

In fact, staffing is a major challenge across the board for the solo firm or for the 500+ staff firm. There isn't a week that goes by where an attorney doesn't ask me where to find specialized individuals to help them with their firm.

When they finally find someone, they have trouble keeping them around because if that person is good, other companies will come in and sweep them away. I've devised an approach based on the high-tech industry to prevent such situations and you'll read about it as you continue with the book.

CHAPTER 02

Vital Steps Necessary for "Tuning Up" Your Practice

Before trying to make any major changes or alterations to your company the first step is to understand where you are at and draw out standard operating procedures to get to where you want to be. I do this through a process that I coined "The Vital Practice Tune-Up".

It's the first thing I do when I enter an organization and it is without a doubt the most essential part of growing a practice. I begin by checking every aspect of the organization ranging from pinpointing referral sources and different lead generators, all the way to ensuring the staff is properly placed whether they are in house or outsourced.

I do a complete evaluation of the practice, in the categories that I spell out below. My aim is to understand who comprises the staff, what numbers drive the finances, what has worked historically, what is working currently and what's missing.

We address each aspect systematically, one by one, and then establish a priority of what to fix first. My scenario follows what a mechanic would do for a car tune-up.

Step 1: Case Management ("Checking the Engine")

Checking the engine means checking your case management system to figure out what its true purpose is and how to configure it appropriately to streamline your operations and expand your practice. This includes integrations, customizations, and full automation.

Step 2: Lead and Client Acquisition ("Check Your Horsepower")

The horsepower of your practice is pinpointing how you generate clients and finding out how to tune your car to add some extra horsepower along the way. I want to know what method you are using to get clients: whether it's through referrals, advertising, marketing, social media, and so on.

Your practice's horsepower basically determines how efficient you are at generating new leads at an affordable and consistent cost.

Step 3: Image ("Turn Heads When You Drive-By")

How does the outside world see your firm? What does your online presence, testimonials, reviews, directory listings, etc. say about you? This category basically creates the image of your law practice from the outside. It does not matter what the size of your firm is, the image can show you how others view your business, and this is essential for branding and gaining traction in the already oversaturated legal market.

Step 4: Budgeting ("Plan an Annual Trip")

This category covers budgeting. It looks at the cost of staffing, marketing, social media, advertising, technology, staff compensations, incentive programs, benefit programs, and whatever else is required to keep your law practice moving. We work everything into your budget and do 12 to 14 months of forecasting.

Step 5: Resource Planning ("Fluid Levels")

Most of the time, attorneys react to problems they face only after they've happen. They often have a bunch of cases to handle; they don't have enough staff, which leads to them scrambling to patch holes. They end up overworking themselves and their staff and I've noticed a swift decrease in quality of service offered when attorneys become overwhelmed.

Advanced resource planning means understanding your operations inside and out, helping you to use your resources and allocate them properly to see a positive return on the number of clients you can acquire in any given month.

Step 6: Outsourcing ("You Don't Always Need to be in the Driver's Seat to Give Directions")

A lot of the work that a firm does lies outside the core of a law practice and can be done by external resources. With today's availability of Virtual Legal Staffing, most of these positions can be outsourced to dedicated virtual staff that are affordable and can be integrated as part of your practice at a very low cost. The roles that can be overtaken by Virtual Staff are as follows,

- Intake Staff
- Admin/Receptionist
- Medical Records/ Document retrieval
- Case management
- Lien negotiations
- Demands Writing
- Investigation
- Client Advocate
- Marketing Staff (Virtual Staff)

This expertise does not need to reside within the firm, and outsourcing can reduce the cost of operations and increase the effectiveness of those programs.

Step 7: Law Practice Development ("Accessories or a New Model")

Every law practice needs to have a practice development plan. If the law practice doesn't expand and grow, it becomes obsolete.

Law practice development starts with a three-year expansion plan. This can be in the same practice area or new practice areas. We have seen the most success with our three-year expansion plan when attorneys are willing to acquire other firms, partner with other solo practitioners or medium-sized firms or expand their network of service providers.

Step 8: Client Retention, Remarketing, and Brand Awareness

Client retention is simultaneously the biggest opportunity and the biggest issue within firms. Very often we see lawyers take their clients for granted, incorrectly assuming that just because they have helped a client in the past, they are locked in to working with that client for the foreseeable future.

With the power of social media platforms, and the traction many attorneys are getting with their lucrative ad campaigns, it is no longer the case that a client will run back to the same attorney who assisted them in the past.

The risk of losing clients that you have assisted in the past can be offset by doing monthly surveys of your existing clients and making sure you're providing outstanding service, all the way from case retention to settlement. I would recommend hiring a Virtual Legal Associate who has the sole job of calling all your past clients and reassuring them that you are still ready to assist them with any legal matter they may have and asking for testimonials if they were happy with your services rendered.

Additionally, planning monthly firm newsletters and SMS broadcasting to existing or past clients (and past leads) for national events, holidays, their birthdays and case settlement anniversaries, will help remind them that you are still active and still hungry to fight on their behalf. You can get a great number of referrals from past clients simply by being present on an ongoing basis. See how your clients rate your services and avoid "guessing their satisfaction level".

MONTHLY INTAKE SURVEY

CLIENT FEEDBACK REPORT

8-10	352 Responders
5-7	52 Responders
0-4	65 Responders

Total Rating from 0 to 10 — Total Responders

MONTHLY TREATMENT SURVEY

CLIENT FEEDBACK REPORT

Very Satisfied	77 Responders
Satisfied	53 Responders
Neither satisfied nor dissatisfied	31 Responders
Dissatisfied	4 Responders
Very Dissatisfied	5 Responders

Satisfaction level — Total Responders

MONTHLY SETTLEMENT SURVEY

CLIENT FEEDBACK REPORT

8-10	103 Responders
5-7	15 Responders
0-4	30 Responders
N/A	5 Responders

Total Rating from 0 to 10 — Total Responders

Based on client survey results, the Law Firm can diagnose what the most important problem in each division is and figure out a solution to resolve it for better client satisfaction. This leads to more positive client reviews and more referrals for the firm. Also, this is a long-term investment strategy for the law firm's brand reputation.

Step 9: Technology Meets Law

Technology is another area where law firms that have been around for 20-30+ years significantly fall behind. It's almost as if, unless pressured to change, they're willing to stay with fax machines and pagers forever! They'll never migrate and are often stuck in their archaic ways.

Firms have a laundry list of technology available to them for automation, client retention, and case management yet they become complacent and fear change. Just to list a few benefits, I have provided below the technology essentials for a modern-day law practice.

Case management, document management, and due date tracking systems are beneficial for the following reasons:

- Advanced communication systems
- Automated website analytics reporting
- Live chat systems
- Custom law firm mobile apps
- Lead management and automated reporting systems
- Automated lead and client follow-up systems

- Automated client surveys and reviews collection systems
- Electronic retainers
  and many more ...

Step 10: Principal Case Management and Review

One of the more pressing issues I've come across over my years in the legal industry is watching many managing attorneys fail to do proper case review sessions with their team. This means they don't use a very structured approach with their staff to truly evaluate the cases that the firm is handling.

I propose setting up weekly, biweekly, or monthly case review sessions. To complement this process, you select for example the 10 highest valued clients or cases, 10 of the most problematic cases, and 10 of the newest sign-ups.

During the review process, you ensure that you're dedicating most of your attention to the 10 most valuable cases, discussing and addressing the problematic cases, and that you are getting a good read on the new incoming cases. This is how you can ensure you are on top of what is going on with your cases and what settlements you can expect. Also, your staff is motivated and obligated to pay attention to details of cases as they know you are auditing and supporting them and not just accepting any case settlement offer. Based on your attention to case status, case value and schedule going forward, you can develop a financial goal for your team. Creating a target for your team also involves creating an incentive program for all your staff. This way everyone is focused and incentivized to achieve the firm's financial goals.

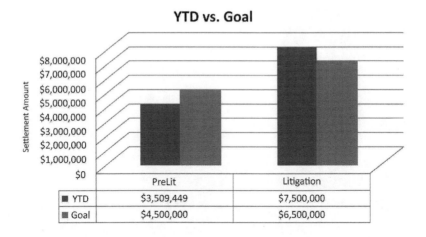

YTD vs. Goal

	PreLit	Litigation
■ YTD	$3,509,449	$7,500,000
■ Goal	$4,500,000	$6,500,000

Step 11: Human Resource Management

Finally, as mentioned many times in this book, the biggest asset of your law practice is your staff. As a service provider, you are marketing your staff's time to your clients. To provide the best service possible, you need a specific job description for each member of the staff as well as proactive annual performance reviews.

Employees should not have to run after attorneys because they haven't had a performance review in 18 months, or a salary increase in the past three years. Especially if they see partners and attorneys make more and more money every year, while their salary remains the same. It creates resentment, which makes it significantly more likely that they will leave the firm for the first offer they get from another firm. Keep your good staff happy by providing a periodical incentive program, and don't be CHEAP when rewarding them for meeting their incentives. Additionally, don't hesitate to terminate unproductive staff; you are not doing them a favor by keeping them around and you are hurting your firm more than you can imagine.

CHAPTER 03

How to Scale a Modern Law Practice

To scale your law practice, you first must look at how you manage and handle clients and their cases.

You need to have an optimized case management system where any stage of client management can be automated.

Whether you're looking to purchase a case management system, or you have one in use already, you need to answer a few questions:

- Is it the right case management software for your practice area(s)?
- Is it configured and operating properly?
- Is it set up for process automation?
- Is your staff trained to use the system properly?
- Are you able to get timely reports that help you make management decisions?
- Can you integrate other needed technologies into your case management system?

(Other needed technologies such as communication systems, lead management, referral systems, document collections, calendaring, reminders, and so on.)

A critical item in case management that managing attorneys often overlook and mismanage is caseload per staff. In most law firms, we see the extreme in which employees either have too few cases or are overwhelmed with an abundance of cases that they cannot manage.

The right case management system allows you to manage this through what is called load-balancing. It ensures that everyone has an adequate load of work or cases.

Leveraging Your Staff

Finding professional, result-oriented staff is a hard enough challenge, but if you have enough employees and don't leverage them appropriately, your staffing problem doesn't disappear.

What makes good staff? Now beauty is in the eye of the beholder, but from my perspective, professional, results-oriented staff are the ones that are both qualified and educated on their role in the company. They are properly trained in their specific role.

Please note that a qualified employee is not always one with a degree. Many individuals can simply read a book, pass a test, and get some sort of certificate.

Employees need to have the right chemistry to fit within the firm. Every practice has a culture that comes from the founder and the people who were there first.

When bringing new employees into a firm, the chemistry and the culture must fit. Otherwise, you can acquire the most qualified person on the market, yet they won't last more than a month in the firm because there is no cultural fit.

Leveraging your staff means finding the best match, not just for the job, but for the practice itself. If a managing attorney is very hands-on and micromanages, new employees must fit within that environment. Similarly, an employee who wants a lot of direction won't fit well with a firm where managers are completely hands-off and expect their staff to be autonomous and self-directed.

Suppose you have two licensed attorneys that come from the same school with the same degree. One will fit well within the first culture, the other won't, and vice versa.

This cultural fit is not limited to the attorneys, but also to receptionists, case managers, and paralegals. Everyone must match the practice culture.

An example scenario: A very ambitious applicant applies for a basic job in a law firm but wants to become a senior paralegal in two years. He/She gets hired as a receptionist and despite all their hard work they will never grow and will remain answering phones for three years after they started, leading them to be miserable.

Whereas, that same person in a different firm, one year later can be the best paralegal the firm has ever had.

Leveraging your staff is also about knowing who they are, what motivates them, and their life goals. All of this allows you to direct them and put them on the right track inside your organization for a long-term win-win experience.

When I interview applicants, I always ask them what their long-term goals are. I ask them to disregard the job and to tell me personally, where they want to be three years from now. It's a standard question, but if the candidate has no prepared answer, it can be an important insight that should not be overlooked.

Sometimes, candidates apply for an interview for a specific job, but I may place them in a different position after the interview because I don't want them to have to just have a job, I want them to have a career.

"I don't want them to just find a job,
I want them to find a career."

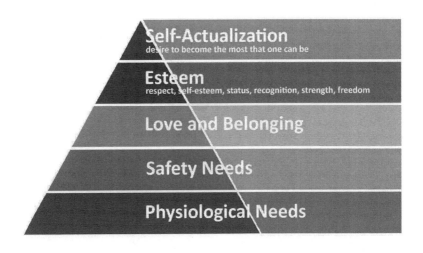

According to Maslow's hierarchy of needs, we also notice that every staff member is capable and has the desire to get to the self-actualization phase once their basic growth needs are met. In a law firm, solely paying a salary and providing benefits is not going to be enough. Career growth structure needs to be pre-planned along with the implementation of incentive programs for staff at every level. This is necessary to help every individual experience their growth and ultimately this will result in the law practice's growth.

Once I hire them, I want them to stay around, and one of the key strategies is to provide them with continuous training.

Investing in your staff should be at the top of your priority list because by investing in your staff you're also investing in your firm. The more you develop your staff the more value you get out of them. It's important to never ignore their training needs as you evolve. Create a career growth path for them through continuous education and certificate programs.

Listening to your staff is a key element of this investment. Listen to what they have to say and keep an open line of communication for them to tell you what is going well and what isn't.

When they have suggestions and ideas, let them be implemented. Shooting down these ideas kills innovation within the firm. However, letting people implement their ideas will make them more invested in the outcome of the firm and ultimately its success.

Employees should be incentivized whenever the firm is incentivized. When the owner or the managing attorney is incentivized, employees should also be incentivized because they hold a share in the practice.

All employees should benefit from the outcome of a case, from the person who first talked to the client to the attorney who wins the trial. So the outcome needs to be visible and shared with everyone, irrespective of their role within the practice.

For example, if the attorney gets a $10,000 bonus for settling the case, the receptionist should also receive a financial bonus. Owners should not take for granted that the receptionist is doing their job answering calls and managing the client, while the attorney is trialing the case. It's unfair that the winning attorney gets incentivized for making a big win, but the receptionist gets nothing.

Incentivizing individuals when the firm succeeds also helps with team building. When a firm meets set objectives, usually financial ones, everybody gets a bonus. It sets a common objective for everyone, and they are incentivized to make the firm more successful so they can make more money too.

If some employees see that every year, they get a 3% or 5% raise while the person they're working with is getting a 10X raise, it will lead to resentment.

I'm not saying that if one person gets a $25,000 bonus, everyone should get that same bonus. The bonus aligns with their respective roles in different divisions within the firm.

Everybody understands that the higher positions who work on cases and have a direct impact on the settlements will get larger bonuses (the attorney makes more than the case manager, who makes more than the receptionist) but at least, everybody shares in the firm's successes. If one person makes all the money and everyone else gets nothing, it doesn't work.

One of the primary drivers for incentivizing is to reduce or eliminate turnover. And the incentives are motivation to help everyone in the firm succeed. When one person succeeds, everybody succeeds and gets a reward.

Incentive Program For Law Firm Employees

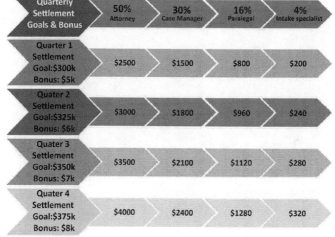

Quarterly Settlement Goals & Bonus	50% Attorney	30% Case Manager	16% Paralegal	4% Intake specialist
Quarter 1 Settlement Goal:$300k Bonus: $5k	$2500	$1500	$800	$200
Quater 2 Settlement Goal:$325k Bonus: $6k	$3000	$1800	$960	$240
Quater 3 Settlement Goal:$350k Bonus: $7k	$3500	$2100	$1120	$280
Quater 4 Settlement Goal:$375k Bonus: $8k	$4000	$2400	$1280	$320

Optimize Workflow Processes

An optimized workflow process means that every step that can be automated, is automated. It starts with getting that initial retainer signed, all the way to disbursement of settlement.

Each step is clearly defined and has a performance metric to create optimal outcomes. The performance metrics include all the checks and balances and possible what-if scenarios.

One typical example where process optimization yields benefits is the number of people touching a case, essentially when dealing directly with the client. In many situations, a lot of redundancy could be eliminated to streamline the process. It increases the outcomes and the value of the case while speeding up the process from sign-up to disbursement.

Lead Generation and Leads Conversion

There are traditional ways of generating cases. The first is word of mouth referrals. That's often how attorneys begin their practice.

After a while, this source dries up and they look at doing basic advertising. Most of it is unproductive because it's not well thought out. They also don't have a consistent budget for advertising.

Many attorneys who still rely on traditional marketing put up a billboard and expect to get a substantial number of cases after a few weeks. It doesn't work like that.

Similarly, law firms can't just throw $5,000 into online advertising and expect to receive 100 retained cases. When they don't get the results they expect, it really turns them off and they decide not to advertise again, or they switch to another agency or marketing area.

They see it as a waste of money that doesn't work. But after a while, they become desperate and try again. Except that this time, they put in $10,000 or $20,000 and still yield the same results.

Or even worse, they get lucky and get a huge case, being led to believe that it was because they spent more, when in reality, it was coincidence.

While that's the trend in many legal firms, there is a systematic road to generating and retaining clients. It's multifaceted. It's not just doing one thing; it's considering and implementing many factors to get the best result.

Remarketing Strategy for Consistent Referrals from Past Clients

One way as mentioned is to *systematically* **get referrals** from previous clients. To accomplish this, firms must remain in continuous contact with old clients and leads. They can do this by remarketing plans through newsletters and SMS broadcasts for holiday greetings, case anniversaries, birthdates, and so on.

Organic Leads by Online Presence Management

Another hidden opportunity to organically generate cases is through your structured **online presence**. Once again, it's not about doing a single activity, it's a combination of marketing vehicles such as updating the website and Google My Business profile, SEO on web pages, and consistent social media professional activities.

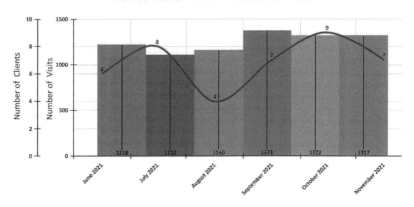

Website Visits and Generated Clients

When it comes to social media, you need to determine when it makes sense to invest in branding for your firm. While Facebook and Instagram may be the most popular platforms, you should also look at others such as LinkedIn, YouTube, TikTok, and so on. In today's day and age and for the foreseeable future, you can't ignore social media. By properly utilizing social media, you are doing something that was near impossible a couple decades ago, low-cost, effective marketing. With only one viral post, a law firm can skyrocket in popularity at little to no cost, bringing in clients of all calibers.

Lead Generation and Advertising Companies

In addition to utilizing social media to expand your law practice, you can also leverage **lead generation companies** and maximize your purchases of PPC and PPL leads. Now this process can be very tricky because it requires not only a consistent budget, but you also have to have patience and wait for your leads to materialize. In addition to consistency and patience, it is essential that your law firm builds an internal infrastructure to handle and convert the leads in a timely fashion.

The typical conversion rate from buying leads can be 6% to 7% but to secure these six or seven solid leads, you first need to go through 93 awful ones. This is where most law firms fail and where I've seen the least amount of patience. Most law firms don't like to play the waiting game and are quick to dismiss a lead source if they're not meeting their extremely high expectations. I think of it like this. If you were certain that going through 100 leads would yield at minimum one 7 figure case, how quickly would you go through those leads to find that 1 singular case? The answer is unanimous, you would go through them VERY FAST, and VERY EFFICIENTLY.

Most law firms are not patient enough and are too quick to move onto "the next big thing" before truly maximizing what they have in front of them.

When attorneys buy leads, they expect a certain number of cases and think that those cases are going to be the difference-maker in the firm, when in reality, if you don't have the necessary intake tools set up, trained intake specialists, or a team to do proper follow ups, even ten, 7-figure cases won't put your name on the map.

Accomplishing successful lead conversions requires up-to-date technological and financial tools and proper internal structure.

Most of the time, lead generation companies get blamed for the poor quality of leads. More than half of the time the blame lies with the law firm's poor intake department that is ill prepared to do the required work to secure cases.

Referral Network

Last but not least, one of the most overlooked yet lucrative ways of increasing case generation is by **strengthening your relationships** with your current referral sources. Many companies don't cultivate these relationships and they end up missing out on potential cases that they could acquire at virtually no initial cost.

Here is a scenario to better understand what strengthening your relationships means. Imagine you have a friend who decides that every time your birthday comes around, they will gift you a watch valued at $10,000 or greater. How would you view this person and how strong do you think your relationship must be for them to casually give you such an expensive gift on your birthday? The answer is, you'd view this person very favorably and you would assume that your relationship is very strong and one of a kind. I mean how often are you getting a gift valued at $10,000? Rarely. In almost all cases, you would assume that you are closer to this person than even your family, because of how generous they are just once a year.

This is the case for referral sources. When another lawyer or law firm decides to give you a case, there is a high chance it's valued in the thousands, yet most law firms don't show the appreciation necessary for such a high valued "gift". Many owners of legal practices take these referrals as if they are entitled to them or as if they expect such favors/gifts, when in reality, case referrals in many practice areas are equivalent to a gift worth thousands of dollars, one in which you would show immense appreciation and gratitude from under different circumstances. Often, when someone provides a referral, the firm owner thanks them briefly, takes the case, and moves on. Instead, they should imagine that these referrals are equivalent to a friend giving you a thousand-dollar gift and show gratitude accordingly. This is the key to scaling your law practice and building relationships that will inadvertently grow your practice and enhance peer relationships.

How To Increase Net Fees Per Case (If You Bill on Contingency)

To increase fees—especially in cases like employment, personal injury, workers comp—you need to work on these cases like each one is the only one that your law firm is currently handling. Remember, you can't just sit around and expect the value of these cases to increase while you're not putting in the work on your end. Given that these are contingency cases, you need to work with the client and service providers day in and day out to build the value of any given case.

Many firms leave the handling of cases in excess of $50,000 or $100,000 to an inexperienced case manager or even worse, the client themselves, and then wonder why they can't scale and grow their practice. These cases require an incredible amount of attention to detail and specifically, double, and triple checking all collected documentation, completed analysis of treatment schedule and visits if applicable, and everything in between. When you pay very close attention to the progress made on those cases and you figure out the formula of what works and doesn't, you can double or triple the value of the case and your law firm can reap the benefits.

Therefore, it is essential to have case reviews in place to ensure your staff is building the value of a case and not undermining its potential. Don't assume it's happening on its own because it isn't.

How To Reduce the Time from Signup to Settlement

Decreasing the time between sign-up and settlement starts with very tight tracking of cases, utilizing an automated case management system, or knowing how to do it manually if necessary. Each part of the process must get properly dated and tracked to monitor progress, or else you end up running in circles around yourself. Being able to date and age everything allows you to determine when a case needs to go into demand and settlement.

Some things to consider. How long does it take to start treatment after signup? At what point is treatment no longer valuable? Insurance carriers often cap the number of visits, so continuous treatment that is no longer billed just delays settlements while not improving case results.

I've seen situations where clients have stopped treating a case and the case manager doesn't realize it until three months later. The case is parked and nobody's paying attention to it for months on end. This creates cash flow issues for firms dealing with contingencies and must be avoided at all costs.

Constantly monitoring the client's process allows the law firm to streamline their law firm's operations which in turn allows the law firm to build an internal structure suitable for expansion. When the client stops receiving treatment, you must be notified immediately so you can move forward to the next stage of their case without being in limbo. A properly set up case management software can send automatic notifications when clients stop receiving treatment as well as send out demands when there has been a prolonged period of no communication.

CHAPTER 04

Virtual Staff vs. In-House Staff

The scalability of a firm depends heavily on the staff and their capabilities. Often, firms can't scale because they can't find "qualified" staff, or they simply can't afford them.

To address these challenges, we break down the firm's day-to-day tasks and determine which areas could benefit from virtual staffing. Note that virtual staffing and outsourcing (which we cover in the next chapter) are not the same. Virtual staff covers dedicated full-time employees who use your law firm's email domain, phone number, and case management software daily. Outsourcing on the other hand is a paid service provider whose role is to work on a specific task or project as a contractor. In short, your virtual staff is just as much a part of your firm as your in-house staff, while your outsourcer is solely responsible for handling tasks sporadically as they come.

A virtual staff is part of your firm, while outsourcing is when you pay a service provider to do specific tasks.

Now that we understand the difference between hiring a remote virtual staff and paying a service provider to outsource specific projects and tasks, I'd like to touch on some of the benefits of moving forward with full-time virtual staff. For starters, when a law firm decides that they have a position in the firm that they need to fill, the first consideration is finding out where this person lives and deciding if it's worth it to them and the firm, to commute to the office daily. This is huge because you have now narrowed down your pool of candidates from hundreds of thousands to maybe one hundred (if that), and that's not even considering our next point which is "for the work that this employee is doing, can I justify paying them a competitive salary when I know they can go work at 100 different law firms within a 25-mile radius." When considering moving forward with virtual staff, off the bat, you have now opened the pool of candidates capable of filling roles within your firm, without having to worry about pay or commute. Now that we know that we can increase our reach with virtual staff, let me explain how we know that virtual staff work for the legal industry.

Over the past few years because of the pandemic and quarantining, we have now discovered that in many industries and professions, it is no longer a requirement for productivity to have your employees come to the office. We have seen this to be especially true in the legal industry. Now this isn't the case across the board for all practice areas, however I have seen first-hand the effectiveness of law firm employees working from home and I can promise you that in most cases, these employees become far more efficient and can thrive in their remote environment.

Before we continue, as a disclaimer, it is important you keep in mind that shifting from strictly employing in-house staff to getting your feet wet with virtual staff requires flexibility and patience. Once you're ready to take the next steps, start to brainstorm the roles you are looking to fill, and more importantly, the tasks associated with these roles. Once you can decipher what kind of work must be done in the office and what kind of work can be done remotely, you'll be able to start sourcing individuals capable of executing your firm's tasks remotely.

From my experience in the legal industry, almost regardless of law firm size, I have pinpointed a handful of positions and tasks that could and SHOULD be delegated to virtual staff. These positions include a receptionist, intake specialist, junior case manager, document retriever, demand writer, executive assistant, and content creator/social media marketer just to name a few. These positions can be filled by hiring virtual staff from all over the world and at a discounted price in comparison to what you would pay someone locally. For example, virtual staffing for these positions can cost anywhere between $1,700/Month to $2,500/Month, whereas local staff doing identical work would cost anywhere from $3,500 to $4,500/Month. Furthermore, with virtual staff, you save on benefits, employment taxes, office space, parking fees, and so on. So much so, that many of the law firms we've worked with have started with one virtual staff and due to saving so much on employee salary, within one year, they were able to acquire more than 40 virtual assistants. In addition to expanding your candidate pool, growing your practice, and saving money, by hiring virtual staff from around the world, you can source for employees who speak multiple languages, allowing you to cater to a larger clientele base. I'll include below additional benefits not mentioned above.

Some of The Benefits of Hiring Virtual Staff

- Flexible scheduling
  - o Your virtual staff can be scheduled to work on your time zone, at your desired hours, including the weekend and American holidays.

- Incredibly task oriented with skills in cultivating reports and tracking company analytics
- No terminations cost
- No employee benefits
- Inexpensive to add or replace virtual staff
- Completely tracked and managed by automated systems

Call Center vs Your 24/7 Virtual Staff

Law firms traditionally use answering services or call centers to answer calls. The problem with this approach is multifaceted but one big issue is that a faceless and unknown individual is answering on your firm's behalf, minimizing the relationship between the firm and the client. You never know when a six-figure or seven-figure call will try to reach you. People in a call center don't know you or how your firm operates so they are unable to provide the level of support that these types of clients require.

Virtual staffing is a way to replace call centers. With dedicated virtual staff, you can train and incentivize remote workers and instruct them on how to take a lead and properly retain a client for the firm.

Another benefit of working with virtual staff is the flexibility it provides the firm. You can have your virtual staff clock in at any time, clock out at any time, and there are no set or prefixed hours to honor. They can also work on weekends allowing your law practice to be accessible around the clock 24/7.

Additionally, with the savings and flexibility offered, virtual staff can fill positions that firms typically don't have internally. For example, you can hire virtual staff to focus on client retention and act as a client advocate. They can contact clients on a consistent basis and ensure that their needs are being met and that they are happy with the services your firm has offered thus far. In addition to following up with clients, your virtual staff can also collect reviews and testimonials for the firm and maintain a high quality of service at a low cost.

It's no surprise that times have changed and although the legal industry has been hesitant to hire virtual staff in the past, today it seems ridiculous to not give it a go.

In fact, when you consider large corporations like banks or credit card providers, most of the time, when talking to an agent from their call center, you're speaking to someone outside of the company with limited access to its data. It also takes a few levels of escalation before you can speak to someone from inside the company who can assist you with your request. With virtual staff, these issues are almost obsolete as they are dedicated, trained, and are part of the firm.

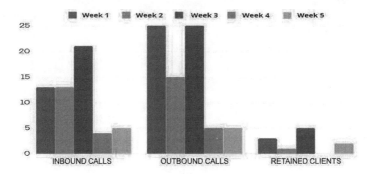

VIRTUAL INTAKE ASSISTANT - MONTHLY PERFORMANCE

CHAPTER 05

Outsourcing

We discussed outsourcing briefly in the previous chapter, but we didn't touch on its benefits and its value-add to many law firms. First off, depending on the law firm and their respective size, some firms just don't need or can't afford a full-time employee. They don't have enough work to justify hiring a full-time demand writer, document collector, accountant, or receptionist, and in these cases, it makes sense to outsource the work when applicable. Many law firms already outsource call centers and answering services, so it shouldn't be a foreign concept to consider outsourcing more administrative tasks or repetitive paralegals tasks.

Breaking Out of The Old Law Firm Model

Traditionally, law practices did everything in-house. When they didn't have the required staff expertise, they hired someone full-time, even if there wasn't enough work to justify that expense.

Today, we recommend that firms outsource client retention, marketing, quality control, and mundane operational work to a trusted service provider. There are legal marketing and practice management[1] companies that offer complete IT package services and can manage law firm website updates, SEO, social media, monthly newsletters, press releases, SMS marketing, client surveys, holiday greetings, and so on.

By outsourcing these types of services, your law firm can reduce staffing costs by two or three times while keeping work production the same. In these cases, you can also leverage the knowledge of a specialist whose primary focus is in a specific line of work. It's also not necessary to have an in-house specialist for legal services such as writing demands, writing motions, or collecting medical records.

Today's law firms must break away from the traditional practice setup and adapt to the times. In a modern practice, you can focus solely on your core competencies. In the legal industry, this would include your attorneys and your senior paralegals.

Everything else could easily and effectively be outsourced or done remotely by a dedicated virtual staff member.

This is the pathway to becoming a completely virtual law firm. Essentially, you have a law firm that consists of 25 staff with no office location other than for legal purposes. You have a few attorneys working from home, a few paralegals doing the same, and everyone else is spread around the globe.

In a traditional firm, everybody commutes to the office, which we've seen to have a negative impact on efficiency and productivity for specific positions. Efficiency and productivity are low while

---

[1] www.legalsoftsolution.com

drama is high. Compensations and benefits are high, and attendance is low.

At some point, you want to give up because you realize that the more people you hire in the office, the more painful the job becomes. So, you'd rather not grow.

Law Firm Organization Chart

Outsourcing Legal Support Services

From a legal service point of view, your law firm can outsource:

- Content writing
- Filling out applications
- Document retrieval
- Identifying expert witnesses
- Writing demands
- Lien negotiations
- Discoveries
- Data backups
- Security setups

- Marketing management
- Online presence management
- Upgrade and maintenance of local systems. (When you have remote people working from home, safety, security, and connectivity can become issues. With outsourced IT services, specialists take care of this for you. You can sleep better at night knowing that your systems are secure, safe, and up to date.)
- HR services that provide termination, compliance, handbooks, hiring contractors, and more. By outsourcing to HR specialists, you reduce your risk of getting employment complaints and lawsuits.

Why You Won't Outsource

The biggest issue with outsourcing services is adoption. It isn't a problem with outsourcing itself, but rather with managers' need for control. They want to be in total control and want to micromanage people by telling them at what time to come in, what time to leave, how to do their work, etc.

Control is a myth. You make yourself believe that you manage everything, but you don't. So you might as well reduce your costs and increase efficiency by outsourcing to experts.

What If You Stick to the Traditional Practice Model?

If you decide to stick with the traditional model instead of adapting to the modern practice model, you will hinder your ability to scale. You will start missing out on certain skill sets because you don't have them in-house. This is especially true with software and technology.

You could easily get employment complaints or complete downtime of your computer systems because nobody upgraded or maintained them. You can also be affected by a virus or other type of malware because you don't have the in-house expertise to prevent those types of attacks.

If one of your employees — like a case manager — is sick for a week, everything slows down during that time.

Outsourcing is one of the first areas to investigate when you're looking to scale, remove headaches, and focus on your core law practice.

Many law practices that decided to go virtual during the COVID-19 pandemic experienced a drastic improvement in the quality of their practice. They eliminated in-house staffing problems such as late attendance, not showing up, early leaves, and many more, while building a core team of virtual staff who were ready to work under any circumstance.

They also no longer had to deal with compensation-related drama, where employees were looking for more money or benefits without understanding the impacts on the law practice.

Owners were also afraid of getting rid of poorly performing employees because of employment law concerns.

With virtual staff and outsourcing, all those problems disappear.

CHAPTER 06

Building Your Referral Network

Referral networks are the most effective way to develop and scale a law practice. Unfortunately, not many attorneys have a structured and organized method of expanding and managing their referral network, and as a result, they struggle with growth.

Regardless of whether you run a small firm or a large firm, there is always a need for a referral network management plan and a referral network manager to execute the plan.

Such a program needs to be structured and have a target list that contains the type of referral sources the firm wants to receive cases from.

- What attorneys do you want to go after? Which service providers?
- What is your value proposition, and why should they work with your firm?
- What types of clients or cases do these sources like to refer to?
- Who or what can you refer to them?

Referrals are bidirectional. Acting as a symbiotic relationship, the art of finding a referral source involves looking for a great set of people to whom you can refer cases to and whom you'd receive cases from.

This is not an automatic process. It requires continuous outreach to your network while managing and updating the status of referred cases. Everyone needs to know where a case stands to ensure nobody feels shorted on fee sharing.

The people who have referred cases to you want to know that you're on top of their cases and their clients. They want to know that you'll hold up your end of the bargain and not tarnish their reputation.

To that end, quality control, status control, and continuous growth are a big part of referral network management.

Referral management also requires a complete incentive program and an appreciation program. This sort of program allows you to show your appreciation to people who refer clients to you. This is very much relationship management and it's essential to growing your firm.

> You can also grow your referral network by increasing your professional contact list. LinkedIn is a great tool for this. When I had about 250 LinkedIn connections, I asked one of my executive assistants to work on expanding my LinkedIn network and work on it for approximately two hours a day. In four months, I went from 250 to 2000 contacts. All these connections

were my target contacts, meaning attorneys. I can now message them, share information, and even recruit them when needed.

Building a referral network is key to your growth and needs to be done as an ongoing project with a plan, deliverables, and proper incentives for the person who is managing that for you.

Setting up a Referral Incentive and Appreciation Program

If you're a solo practitioner and can't afford to hire someone to do the work for you, set aside one day a week to build your referral network and don't quit until you have contacted every worthwhile attorney in your vicinity.

You do this by reaching out to everyone you've ever been in contact with: people you went to school with, previous co-workers, previous employers, and people who have referred clients to you or could refer clients to you in the future. Reach out to them, talk to them, and invite them for coffee, breakfast, lunch, or dinner.

In larger firms, you can hire virtual staff to do this work for less than $2000 a month. With the proper instructions, this person will follow a recipe to develop, manage, and expand your referral network.

The process is simple. Your virtual staff continuously contacts targeted firms and sets up a ten-minute "get to know each other" call with the managing attorney. They will tell your referral prospect that you can send cases their way and vice versa. If your practice is not in the same geographical area, there's no risk of direct competition.

Over time, you build that relationship by putting these contacts on your mailing list. They will receive monthly newsletters from you and when they send you a new referral your referral manager contacts them to show them your appreciation. They will also update them on the case status and the fees. With a fee-sharing agreement in place, they should know when to expect the fee to come in and approximately what it will be.

With a $2000 per month expense, this referral building program can easily generate 10X ROI.

You can't lose with a well-organized and well-managed referral network. It always pays off.

People don't do it because they say they don't have the time for it, or it doesn't fit their personality. That's fine. In that case, get somebody else who has the time and personality for it and ask them to do it on your behalf.

A Note on Fee Sharing:

In most states, attorneys can have a fee sharing agreement or a referral sharing agreement. Each party receives a percentage of net attorney fees or a fixed amount for a referral. This agreement can be between two practicing firms.

On top of that, you can incentivize your virtual referral network manager. For example, you pay them $2000 a month (full time) or $1000 a month (part time), and you give them a $50 bonus for getting a referral agreement in place. Using this approach, you incentivize your referral manager to sign up as many referrals as possible.

Showing Appreciation

Showing appreciation for referrals doesn't have to be complicated or costly. For example, it could be something small like buying their office lunch or sending over a gift basket as a thank you for their assistance and trust in you.

These actions keep the relationship warm. Essentially, you are reaching out to "date" someone else, and after a date or two, you want to build a relationship that works for both of you.

As your firm grows, use a referral tracking management system so you can get reports and statistics over time.

Ask yourself. How much did you make from your referral network? How much did you make from each specific referral relationship?

A tracking system will help you gauge your engagements and identify the ones that work best so you can try to duplicate them. A simple system we use is called 411 referrals.[2] It's a free web-based platform and mobile application to use for any attorney that builds a referral network in which you can manage and track your referral cases.

---

[2]   www.411referrals.com

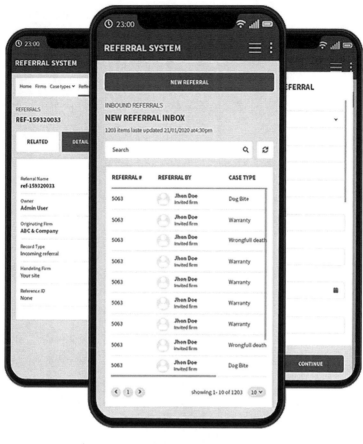

LEGAL REFERRAL APP Available on App Store and
Google Play
www.411referrals.com[3]

---

[3] The Legal Referral App and platform are free to use.

Why More Firms Don't Implement a Referral Program

Attorneys don't implement referral and appreciation programs in their firms because they went to school to become a lawyer and this is not part of a legal education, it's law practice business management so it's often put on the back burner and forgotten.

For a referral program to be successful, it needs to be done very efficiently. Somebody does all the legwork, coordination, and management of the referral then the attorney shows up on a call for ten minutes, builds a relationship with a peer, and goes back to their law practice. It's much more efficient and takes less than fifteen minutes of the attorney's time.

All owners of practices, whether small or large, know that referrals are essential. The only way it'll be executed and managed properly is by assigning the work to virtual staff that are affordable and organized. It's also a great path for growth.

Example Referrals Management Report

Case #	Referrals	Referral Source	Case Type	Client Name	Incident Date	Attorney Fee	Estimated Settlement Fee	Estimated Settlement Date	Case Status	Pay Status
#1	Referred out	Firm 1	PI	Barbara Smith	02/03/21	25%	$800,000	Jun 2021	Settled	Received
#2	Referred out	Firm 2	EM	Joe Smith	06/13/21	26%	$250,000	Oct 2021	Settled	Pending
#3	Referred out	Firm 2	WC	David Taylor	08/28/21	33%	$300,000	Nov 2021	Settled	Pending
#4	Referred in	Firm 1	RS	Adam Brooks	11/23/21	28%	$1,200,000	Mar 2022	Treatment	Paid
#5	Referred in	Firm 3	PI	Mike Chester	07/18/21	20%	$450,000	Dec 2022	Settled	Due

CHAPTER 07

Law Firm Technology

While many industries around the world are using technology to adapt to our changing times, the legal industry is once again falling behind and remaining in their archaic ways. This needs to change. Many solo practitioners and medium-sized firms believe that once you get the lead in, sign them up, and begin working on their case, a Dropbox or a Google drive setup will do the rest. They think that file sharing is essentially the same as automation, and that's where they are wrong.

This type of process does not exist in Dropbox, Google Drive, or any other file-sharing system. Implementing the proper workflow effectively requires having systems in place that streamline the process from beginning to end. Essentially, these systems watch over you and your staff to make sure everything is done properly and on time.

Technology is your best weapon to do workflow process optimization. It works for cases, operations, and marketing. You define the processes you need, then find technologies that help you implement the workflow for each process and finally, you execute.

Case Management Technologies

It begins by having comprehensive client and case management software. It allows you to automate part of the case management process, beginning with the intake. Instead of relying on word documents or online forms, the lead intake information and retainer go directly into the case management system.

The tool helps to open the case and set up all the calendaring and documentation. You can also identify all the important due dates for a case. All this information is linked together automatically for you, and your whole team is therefore granted access and capable of working together through the system.

The same system can generate the forms and letters typically needed during a case. This includes for example, engagement letters to insurance companies or the other party, notifications, etc. Case management system technologies can automate that entire process.

There are template-based systems that can be customized and auto-populated which allow you to proceed very quickly through the intake process, opening the case, and moving on to the next step.

The case management software is the central piece, and you can also leverage the connectivity and integrate it with other tools to automatically get related case information as far as schedules, notes, faxes, texts, calls, and emails. So, when you pull up a client account, any update (data, communication, correspondence, retainers, required signatures, police reports, and any document) from anyone involved in the case is stored in the system and is visible to everyone who is permitted to have access.

The system can also send reminders automatically to another party for scheduled events.

Law Firm Communication Technologies

Today, the most outstanding way of communicating and providing service to clients is having a custom mobile app for your business. Law practice owners or attorneys can also consider having their own custom law firm mobile app. The placement of a law firm mobile app on people's cell phones—especially if it sits on their main screen—is the fastest and easiest way to get case information from clients. Clients can easily submit the intake form and sign the retainer through the app. Law firms can also provide case updates through the mobile app by sending notifications and reminders, collecting required documents, chatting with clients, and so on. Law firms don't need to rely on the old communication methods such as business cards while the young generation is getting ahead by utilizing cell phones.

Law practice business cards have outlived their usefulness. Not only have business cards passed their time, we are noticing that sending people to a law firm's website is similarly seeing decreased utility. To begin, most websites aren't up to date properly to make it easy to navigate and find a way around, so potential clients quickly abort and find the next method of contacting someone to take their case.

There are companies that can create a custom mobile app[4] that can be optimized for all sorts of legal practices. The custom law firm app can help with the following activities:

- Direct communication between the client and the law firm
- Chat with the client
- Get a retainer signed directly through the app
- Collect required documents, which is something most firms struggle with. Using the app, clients can send documents directly from their phones. If they forget, they receive a reminder.
- Provide links to resources
- Provide the latest news about a certain market
- Exchange referrals

---

[4]   https://legalsoftsolution.com/custom-mobile-apps/

On the previous page is an example of the latest and fastest communication method by having a custom Mobile App for your Law Firm. Mobile Apps are downloadable from Google Play and the App Store. From case submission, retaining, and case updates, having it all in one place is very convenient for clients, especially for a younger generation.

Operations Technologies

One of the concerns with dealing with the remote workforce is making sure they are present and doing the work they were hired for. Technology can also help in that regard.

Monitoring and tracking technology can capture periodic screenshots to ensure that remote workers focus on their work. The technology can also record calls, confirm attendance, and monitor many other behavioral aspects that help to determine what a remote worker is doing. It doesn't matter if the person is based in the US or overseas. Everything is manageable via available technologies.

Operation technologies also cover HR. So instead of taking months or years to set up a complete HR function, you can set it up in a matter of days with HR technology. This includes:

- Handbooks
- Training
- Notices and notifications
- Termination
- Corrective actions
- Certificate programs
- Performance review metrics and reports and more.

They can all be automated and streamlined by leveraging the correct technology.

Marketing and Lead Management Technologies

Many firms get leads by purchasing them or generating them directly in house. These leads can be costly and handling them manually is almost impossible.

Lead management systems provide technologies to manage and collect lead information from any source by receiving data from phone calls, submissions, emails, etc. It doesn't matter if it's social media, websites, forums, or pay-per-click advertising. The lead management software can be set up to automatically identify the lead source and lead type and place it in a pre-scheduled automated follow-up sequence. The automated follow-up sequence is essential to building a relationship with the lead to retain their case.

MONTHLY LEAD SOURCE ASSESSMENT REPORT

March 2021	Leads	Requested Refunds	Accepted Refunds	Pending Refund Requests	Net Leads	Cost per Lead	Estimated Total Cost	Total Cost	Cases	Confirmed Cases	Leads Conversion to Cases	Estimated Cost per Case	Cost per Case	Pending Retainers	Refund Rate
LEAD SOURCE 1	5	5	5	0	0	$20	$0	$0	0	0	0%	$0	$0	0	100%
LEAD SOURCE 2	14	10	9	0	5	$50	$250	$250	1	1	20%	$250	$250	0	64%
LEAD SOURCE 3	85	66	57	1	28	$160	$4,320	$4,480	5	5	18%	$864	$896	1	67%
LEAD SOURCE 4	10	8	5	1	5	$225	$900	$1,125	0	0	0%	$0	$0	0	50%
LEAD SOURCE 5	117	97	87	1	30	$400	$11,600	$12,000	0	0	0%	$0	$0	0	74%
LEAD SOURCE 6	107	92	81	1	26	$500	$12,500	$13,000	2	2	8%	$6,250	$6,500	1	76%
LEAD SOURCE 7	18				18	$265	$4,770	$4,770	0	0	0%	$0	$0	0	
LEAD SOURCE 8	0	Not Refundable			0	$325	$0	$0	0	0	0%	$0	$0	0	N/A
LEAD SOURCE 9	5				5	$530	$2,650	$2,650	0	0	0%	$0	$0	0	
TOTAL	361	278	244	4	117	-	$36,990	$38,275	8	8	7%	$4,624	$4,784	2	68%

You can generate an automated text sequence or email sequence from the lead management platform. It can also support automated calls and on-demand calls.

The lead management system is designed to capture and convert prospects and can increase lead conversion by 40 or 50%. Any law practice that spends thousands of dollars on lead generation needs to have such a system in place to get the maximum ROI for its efforts.

As part of marketing management, you can also leverage technology for referral management, as discussed in the previous chapter. Technology allows you to connect and manage all referral sources and referred cases. You can track payments and agreements for those referrals and manage communications and client status updates.

Marketing technology helps automate these aspects of your legal practice:

- Deploy and collect surveys
- Publish newsletters and SMS campaigns

- Publish Press releases
- Collect online reviews and testimonials

To build a modern practice, explore and utilize all the technologies available in other industries that can help you manage and operate your practice. These technologies will reduce your cost of operation and streamline the process from the initial signing of a client to the closing and settlement of the case.

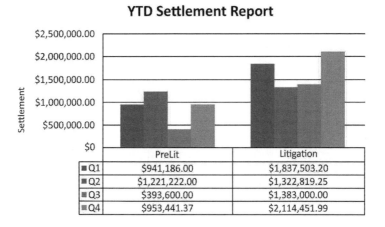

YTD Settlement Report

	PreLit	Litigation
Q1	$941,186.00	$1,837,503.20
Q2	$1,221,222.00	$1,322,819.25
Q3	$393,600.00	$1,383,000.00
Q4	$953,441.37	$2,114,451.99

CHAPTER 08

Marketing & Case Generation

The first step in a successful marketing campaign is to have a plan: a budget, a proper schedule, and then a properly mapped out ROI. In truth, I have yet to work with a law firm that has developed a successful marketing plan on their first go around. Most of what I have seen consists of ridiculous initiatives like "flavor of the month" or "color of the day." Many attorneys will see a colleague put an ad on a billboard and they assume that their massive caseload and success is a direct result of this campaign. So what do they do? They spend thousands and thousands of dollars trying to replicate it. Or in the same token, they will use Facebook or Instagram ads and assume that if a law firm is successful, it is a result of these ad campaigns. Now don't get me wrong, they do play a role, however a far more minute role than you would assume.

If you constantly try to replicate based on exterior facades, you essentially have no plan, no budget, no timeline — hence, no ROI.

Let's start with the three most effective forms of marketing based on my research and analysis: traditional, online, and networking.

You need a marketing plan, regardless of the approach you take. There are too many ways to market, and no company can do them all. So, you need to find what works for your law firm in your specific practice area and focus on something you believe you can excel on, something your competition couldn't replicate regardless of their financial situation. Although billboards may work for some companies, they don't work for most law practices and the trend is slowly diminishing over time. So let's focus on what works in today's day and age.

Traditional Marketing

Traditional marketing consists of:

- Display advertising
- Mailers
- Newspaper
- Radio
- TV

This type of marketing requires initial capital and funds to invest over a long period. You need the patience to wait at least a year to see a return on your investment. This can work for large firms with deep pockets, but for your average solo practitioner drowning in debt and for your small to midsize law firms, this is no longer an option.

Furthermore, traditional marketing requires a certain expertise that most firms don't have. I have seen billboards that cost thousands of dollars per month, but I have not the slightest clue what services they are advertising, where I can contact them, and why I should choose them. They just want to see their pretty face every time they drive to get their morning coffee. The message is lacking, and there is no clear call to action. In these cases, you might as well flush your money down the toilet.

The same goes for radio ads and TV commercials. They are either too long or too short and people have become wary of these advertisers, often believing them to be sleezy or corrupt. There are guidelines to follow when creating these types of advertising but because it is not properly planned or implemented, firms spend a lot of money and receive mediocre or often poor results.

Online Marketing

Online marketing is a vast, unlimited playground. And because there are so many ways to market online, it's easy to get lost and waste a lot of money. That's why funnel marketing is so critical to successful online marketing. It allows you to cast a wide net to find people. Then you focus on the ones who can really utilize your services.

The highest cost of any online marketing is client acquisition.

The cost of a campaign or the cost of getting a lead doesn't matter. If the leads don't convert to clients, they are useless. One lead that generates $50,000 is better than 10,000 leads that generate a dollar each.

To build a solid online marketing plan, you need to know your budget, timeline, and the method you will use. Will it be social media like Facebook and Instagram? Will you be doing text messaging or search pay-per-click?

If you're planning on doing ads, they must be properly designed. Otherwise, you will drown in the crowd. These are highly specialized skills to get the look, the messaging, and the call to action right.

Once you have a lead, you need the ability to track it automatically and trace it back to your marketing campaign. That's how you can calculate the cost of acquiring a client, thus helping you understand your ROI. That's how you can ensure that you're investing in the appropriate online marketing approach.

One advantage of online marketing vs. traditional marketing is your ability to target very specific locations and demographics. You can also test multiple versions of your ads in real-time and adjust them based on results.

It's a type of flexibility you don't have with traditional marketing. When you put up a billboard, you can't change it every month because it's too expensive to do so. But with online marketing, you can make changes with the click of a button.

Additionally, it's important to have somebody on top of your online marketing, so they can continuously tweak any ongoing campaign to get the best results. Don't think you can teach this to yourself overnight and remember that you went to law school to practice the law, not to figure out the algorithms of online marketing.

All practice types do not produce the same results from each online platform. Just because Facebook ads work for a Personal Injury practice does not mean it will also work for Estate Planning.

Platform Recommendations for Each Practice Type:

Personal Injury Ranking of Case Generation

o Potential clients are looking for your services via the search vs. social media push method.
   1. Google Ads
   2. Facebook
   3. Instagram

Estate Planning, Will & Trust, Probate, Tax

o Other professionals are recommending your services for their clients to complete the solution or add protection
   1. Referral Network (CPA's, Wealth Management, Banking, Real Estate Agents, etc....)
   2. Facebook
   3. Instagram
   4. TikTok
   5. Google
   6. Yelp

Employment, Labor, Works Compensation

o You are educating the potential client as to their rights vs. a Google search for people already searching for what they need
   1. Facebook
   2. YouTube
   3. Instagram
   4. TikTok
   5. Google

Criminal, Immigration, Bankruptcy, Probate

o People already know that they need to retain an attorney to help them with the matter and are searching for it directly online.
   1. Google
   2. Yelp
   3. Facebook
   4. YouTube

Other Case Generation Systems

1. Google my business (GMB) at very targeted areas and not competing with metropolitan locations with lots of competition. Focus on small towns within your state.
2. College Campus signage for specific types of practices like Personal Injury.
3. Directory Registration, we deployed a system to register attorneys in over 150 online directories with links back to the firm website.

Networking

I define networking as a combination of using social media and in-person communication to do marketing. It consists of building your network on LinkedIn, attending social gatherings whether you enjoy going out or not, and by being a trustworthy and reliable person that other attorneys and acquaintances would feel proud to send you over a case. If social gatherings and being nice aren't your thing, you can also expand your reach through regular social media postings that are relevant and engaging.

Your practice also requires someone to engage with everyone who connects through your social media profiles. That social media manager can also make sure that you connect to other practices and service providers. That person builds your referral network, as mentioned in chapter six. However, they are much more engaged online. They can create online content on your behalf, such as explanation videos, YouTube content, and more. They approach it on two fronts: professional and personalized. On the professional side, it's more of a wider reach, like service to the community. On the personalized side, it presents you as a regular person, not just someone trying to sell a service. Your social media manager presents the more human side of you and your firm.

Referral networks are best approached to build up the practice, regardless of size or type of practice. We have created a systematic system to build and track referral networks. The best method that has paid off has been hiring a Virtual Staff (Referrals Manager) costing less than $2000 a month for a minimum period of 3 months to perform the following tasks.

1. Create a list of all potential firms that are target referrals sources
2. Create a simple message to ask them to connect with you via LinkedIn
3. Once the connection is made to send them a request for a short conversation with attorney
4. Schedule the short call on your calendar with a quick summary of the scheduled firm and the attorney's bio.
5. Create a referral fee structure (be generous) to offer the targeted firm
6. Virtual Staff then continue to nurture the relationship and referred cases on the ongoing basis.

7. Sending continuous communication, holiday greetings, commenting on social media posts and calls are the best ways to build referral relationships that last. I have experienced building a referral network that counted for over 50% of firm revenue over time.

When working with one of our larger clients, we took over the social media profiles of the attorneys, paralegals, and other members of the staff. Using their profiles, we promoted the law firm through posts that emphasized the firm's work, the employees, and the culture.

CHAPTER 09

Client Retention Program

Don't fall into this trap! A big issue that plagues the legal profession is the fact that after cases are settled and the client and attorney are both happy with the results, over time, law firms begin to forget about former clients. They assume that when clients need legal services, they will automatically return to a firm that helped them before. That might have been the case before, but it's no longer true.

Traditionally, when a client started working with a firm, they remained with them. Just like clients would remain with the same dry cleaner, tailor, or butcher. Now, they choose the one that's most convenient or popular.

Today, there is so much marketing of legal services that clients are tempted to try other services or other organizations. If you expect clients to come back to you two years from now without needing to do anything, you will lose that client.

They will go to other firms who do a better job of pushing their names and relating to your former clients. Doing a great job is not enough to guarantee repeat clients. Other firms will steal them away from you. Just like you would take clients from them if you could…

Be Proactive or Be Forgotten

Building a long-lasting client base requires a lot of hard work and mutual loyalty. You need to be proactive and build a strategy to remain in touch.

There are several effective approaches you can use to remain on the top of your former clients' minds:

- Remember and send personalized birthday wishes. This can be scheduled years in advance and is always a welcome surprise… if it doesn't look like a standard greeting that you would send to anyone.
- Send personalized holiday greetings to the clients or their spouse. Showing care for other members of your client's family also puts you in a favorable position when they need legal help.
- Send personalized anniversary recognitions. For example, if someone received a sizable settlement, you could send congratulations and reminders on the anniversary of the settlement.
- Monthly newsletters that provide news about the practice, changes in the law that may affect or interest them, new services, new locations, etc.
- Do good deeds or make donations that you publicize to your clients. It shows that you are a real person doing work that helps the community.
- Use a mobile App to stay connected and communicate with your former client and provide case updates.

- Ask your Virtual Assistant to comment on former clients social media on your behalf to maintain the relationship.
- Asking for a good Google Review or Testimonials followed by an application gift card or letter works great.

With regular outreach, former clients regularly hear from you. Whenever they have a need, your name will come to mind first because, over time, you've built trust with them.

CHAPTER 10

Budgeting & Finance

You aren't running a law firm. You're running a business, and businesses need to have finances that come from planning and forecasting.

You need monthly, real-time P&L reports. You also need a twelve-month budget for everything from staffing to marketing to advertising. With the twelve-month plan and forecasting, your P&L report will tell you where you stand and the state of your cash flow. Many law practices don't have these systems and plans in place, so they either feel like they're doing well or doing terribly based on a gut feeling. They also think that their only financial obligation is to do their yearly taxes.

Most firms have a CPA who does a generic P&L report every month or every other month. There is little thought behind the report and no analysis. It consists of reconciling the numbers for the end-of-year report and tax filings. That's the extent of their financial planning.

Plan for Project Spending

Planning is looking ahead, not looking at the past. If you plan to hire new employees, or spend more on advertising and marketing, you need to know whether you'll have the money for it. That information comes from the P&L report.

However, you still need to track income and fees to see whether you can spend more money on advertising, marketing, building an incentive program, or any other project that requires a financial investment.

At the beginning of every year, I conduct an exercise where we do a complete revenue projection for the year. We then create an incentive program based on the revenue projections. For example, if we forecast $200,000 in incentives to attorneys and staff, we need to make sure that the budget allows for it.

The same goes for marketing and advertising. If you plan on spending $20,000 per month on a marketing campaign, you need to budget for it. Otherwise, you might end up spending the $20,000 on something else and no longer have it for the campaign. Forcing you to have to stop your campaign.

Operate your firm like a true corporation, creating an annual budget to include the major expenses such as:

- Staffing
- Marketing
- Advertising
- Insurance
- Rent

- Office Expenses
- Continued Education
- Travel
- Incentive Programs

Ask your accountant to produce a monthly P&L in a timely manner on the 15th of each month. This is what you are paying them for. Not once a year when it is too late to take any action or to expand or cut back. Most firms take this very lightly and become a victim of financial mismanagement. Every time I ask a firm for a financial statement, they have to ask the accountant for a simple report that should have been provided monthly and analyzed by the firm's principal employees. They have no idea what the numbers are.

"KNOW YOUR NUMBERS IN REAL-TIME"

Real-Time Reporting

The solution to avoid these problems is to conduct real-time reporting by forecasting actuals and distributions.

Any bookkeeper that understands ongoing bookkeeping financials that aren't only for the sake of taxes can help. But when owners get a P&L, they need to understand it. If they don't understand it, they need to find somebody who will.

Many owners collect P&Ls and put them in a drawer without ever looking at them. To them, it's just a lot of mumbo-jumbo.

But the numbers are essential to do adequate planning. For example, here is a sample distribution for a law firm that receives $5 million in settlements per year.

Settlements		$5,000,000.00
Revenue	50%	$2,500,000.00
Attorney Fees	20%	$500,000.00
Marketing	5%	$125,000.00
HR	15%	$375,000.00
Office Automation	10%	$250,000.00
Salaries and Benefits	25%	$625,000.00
Net Profit	25%	$1,250,000.00

Each line identifies what portion of the settlements goes toward a budget category to ensure proper funding during the year.

While this table illustrates yearly revenue, you could use the same model for individual settlements. So 5% of a $250K settlement goes to marketing, 10% to office automation, and so forth.

With such a plan in place, you know how much revenue you need to generate to cover your yearly obligations. For example, if 25% of your revenue goes toward salaries and benefits, and your total yearly payroll is $400K, you know that you need $1.6M in revenue, so $3.2M in settlements.

CHAPTER 11

Business Development

Lead and marketing generation is a daily operational activity. Business development turns to the future.

Business development looks three to five years ahead, while lead generation looks three to five months (or even weeks) ahead. It covers aspects of your business such as:

- How will you expand your practice?
- What offices can you open in other locations?
- Will you expand into another state or manage a multi-state practice?
- Will you expand into new practice areas (e.g., adding personal injury if you're already working in employment)?
- Will you partner up with other firms?

Business development looks at large, strategic objectives and does not focus so much on tactics. The tactics come later.

Incubate Like Silicon Valley

When it comes to innovation, firms can look to the high-tech industry for successful models. For example, large firms could use incubation as a growth strategy. This is how companies like Google and Amazon scale so quickly and efficiently.

Google has a building dedicated to incubation. They take new graduates with fresh ideas they've been working on in their homes, then bring them into their environment and provide them with resources such as HR, marketing, and financing. In return for the incubation resources, the graduates give a percentage of the company to Google. If any of those projects make it big, Google stands to make a tidy profit.

We have implemented a similar approach with firms that had extra unused space in the building. They look for new attorneys who have recently passed the Bar or have been practicing for less than a year and are finding it difficult to build their business.

The firm brings in these attorneys and provides them with business and legal mentorship. In exchange for a 10-30% interest in their practice, the larger firms build up the smaller ones. Once the new attorney becomes successful, they can launch their new firm, and the incubator becomes a 10-30% partner of a growing business.

With each new launch, you can do more incubation. It's an innovative and modern way of doing business development in the legal industry.

However, don't expect to see a ROI for three to five years. You're building for the future.

Retired Attorneys

Traditionally, when attorneys, doctors, and lawyers retire after 30 or 40 years, they wind down their practice, let people go, and wait until the lease is over. At that point, they close the office, put all the documentation in storage, and go home.

Basically, they're throwing away thirty to forty years of hard work, blood, sweat, and tears. This doesn't happen in other businesses. Before going into retirement, the owners sell the business instead of closing it. They don't want to throw away forty years of effort.

We've successfully implemented an approach with attorneys who are near retirement. We approach firms where the owner is nearing retirement.

Then we create a program for them where a newer firm takes over the older firm's practice, gets rid of the overhead, and installs an exclusive referral agreement with the old firm. Any new business that comes into the old firm gets handled by the new firm. The old firm remains in place but acts more like a shell corporation.

The new firm revives the old firm's online presence, remodels the website, and reaches out to former clients to get more business.

In return, the retiring attorney gets a referral fee—indefinitely.

With this approach, one of our clients has made more net income from referral fees in retirement than he did in his 38 years of practice.

> An attorney couple also implemented this system at retirement. Unfortunately, the husband passed away one year into the program. The wife was not financially secure at the time. She now has a solid and steady retirement income from the ongoing referral fees.

When you look at other industries, you can find many novel ways to develop your business beyond the traditional takeover or buyout approach. The examples in this chapter are not new for other industries, but they are foreign to most legal practices.

With the proper setup and automation, you can expand through partnerships and novel profit-sharing agreements. Everybody wins, and you grow your practice with minimal overhead and headaches.

UBE Expansions: (Uniform Bar Exam)

Utilizing and staffing attorneys who have passed the UBE exam (42 States nationwide).

You can find out more about states who participate in this program from: https://www.ncbex.org/exams/ube/

This method enables your firm to eventually practice in 42 states as a State Licensed Attorney, not motioned in or "use bar admissions in other states to "waive" into the bar" another old method is also **reciprocity.**

I have worked with countless firms over the past couple of years who have expanded their practice in over 8 states by taking the UBE and essentially becoming an attorney who can now service on average 2 new states a year.

You simply use your current location as practice headquarters that essentially handles all operational aspects of your practice, including Lead Generation, Marketing, Accounting, Finance, HR, and case management services. The only difference is that you now have an attorney that is not limited to one or 2 states.

Some states require a physical presence in the state which can easily be established by leasing a space in a professional building like Regus at a very affordable rate.

We have created a nationwide Consumer Protection Firm (Lemon Law) utilizing this method and in 18 months generated over 150 cases while growing on average 50% every six months in case volume.

CONCLUSION

Running a law firm today is more challenging than ever. At the same time, there is more opportunity to create a firm that grows and scales profitably than could even be imagined by attorneys just one generation ago.

Here are the fundamental principles I leave you with that we discussed in this book.

The path from a stupid to intelligent Law Practice:

1. Review and monitor your numbers
2. Create and manage your firm's KPIs
3. Evaluate and optimize your processes
4. Incentivize your team for top performance
5. Know your clients and their case statuses
6. Maintain and monitor your team's quality of work
7. Outsource often
8. Nurture your networking relationships
9. Maximize your virtual staffing team to reduce cost and scale up
10. Utilize technology and automation in your firm
11. Understand and monitor your case cost in real-time

Finally, always think outside the box, surround yourself with excellence and avoid mediocrity.

After working with law firms of all sizes and in virtually all practice areas, I have proven that by applying modern business approaches to the practice of law it is possible to build a law firm that fulfills your desire for financial freedom and time freedom–something rarely achieved in a professional practice.

By eliminating a multitude of problems that firms face internally and operationally it is possible to grow your firm predictably.

My hope is that this book opens your eyes to new possibilities for growing and scaling your firm; that your ambitions are raised and that you aspire to build a truly remarkable law firm.

My team and I are standing by, ready to help you fulfill your vision for your modern law firm. When you're ready for help, reach out to me:

https://legalsoftsolution.com/
Phone: (424) 341-4917
Email: support@legalsoftsolution.com

Hamid Kohan

Made in the USA
Middletown, DE
24 October 2024